VICTORY WITH A WARRIOR'S MENTALITY: SUCCESS IS COLOR BLIND

Copyright © 2025 by Frank McClure

All rights reserved. No part of this publication may be reproduced, distributed or transmitted in any form or by any means, including photocopying, recording, or other electronic or mechanical methods, without the prior written permission of the publisher, except in the case of brief quotations embodied in critical reviews and certain other noncommercial uses permitted by copyright law.

Victory with Warriors Mentality: Success is Color Blind / Frank McClure
Hardback: 979-8-9942831-0-3
Paperback: 979-8-2954-7451-4
eBook: 979-8-9942831-1-0

DEDICATION
1 JOHN 5:7

I dedicate this book to the Holy Trinity—the Father, the Son, and the HolySpirit. To my late wife, Jymmie Jackson McClure, whom God blessed to love for over 46 years, and for blessing us with a wonderful family. Jymmie was my steadfast companion in faith and career, providing unwavering support.

I also dedicate this book to my late children, Derek Caldwell McClure and Jennifer Hall Allison. Derek was an energetic son with multiple God-given gifts, who passionately shared his testimony for the Lord Jesus Christ. Jennifer possessed a quiet, humble spirit that illuminated every room.

Additionally, I dedicate this book to my children, Jara, Frances, and Tony, as well as my grandchildren and great-grandchildren. And to my son in law William Smith And to my Beloved sister, Doris McClure Williams, who is greatly missed. To Stephanie Walker who assisted to make the transcript and book possible.

To my beloved parents, Paul McClure and Cornelia McClure, who worked tirelessly to support fourteen children, I dedicate this book. By the power of the Holy Spirit, I stand on their shoulders and the unwavering support of my family, a legacy captured in our family album and within these pages. Love is family, and to possess both is a divine blessing. Without God and my family, this faith journey would have been impossible. To God be the glory. 2 Corinthians 9:15, Psalm 103:17-18.

VICTORY WITH A WARRIOR'S MENTALITY: SUCCESS IS COLOR BLIND

I am Frank McClure, born October 25, 1944, in York County, South Carolina, during the Jim Crow era. I was eleventh of the fourteen children of Paul and Cornelius McClure.

As I look back over my life, I now awaken every morning with a victorious mentality. My thinking perspective and attitude toward others is filled with love which has changed my attitude and the way I respond to others and situations. I have been transformed with a new mindset, and it gives me a new look at life and love for all mankind.

The new mentality inspires me to be positive and focused on teamwork. The transformation of my mind has influenced how I handle situations. As I encounter situations now, I've learned that a winning mindset is needed to prepare properly.

I look at being a victorious warrior in the context of winning and also as a former athlete. I have been seasoned with travel opportunities to observe many professional teams. The Golden State Warriors Basketball Team stands out. This team is the epitome of what it means to have a victor's mentality; they go beyond simply winning games and championships. The Golden State Warriors embody a specific approach called teamwork.

I like the fact that when an individual with a victor's mentality suffers a loss, they don't see it as the end, but as an opportunity for bigger victories. Unfortunately, I didn't have that type of mindset years ago. I lost many opportunities to better myself and family.

I remember losing my job at CDA Textile in 1964, while my wife was pregnant. Deacon Thomas Garvin wrote me a letter of encouragement filled with great advice. That advice helped get me back on track. During that time, I needed much encouragement, and the letter helped to make sure that I never strayed too far from my path. (Isaiah 42:10-13)

This was an awareness from God, not a loss. God has transformed me with a new mindset, a victorious mentality (Romans 12:2).

I was not aware of the two types of mentalities. Reading further, you will have the opportunity to explore the one-sided mentality which I had. I thank God for His regeneration of a spiritual mindset, changing my worldly mindset to one that is aligned with God's will. It fundamentally changed my thinking and perspective. All of this inspired my spirit with a new mindset. (Ephesians 4:23).

Before being transformed and maturing as a young person, at the height of the Jim Crow era, I was dealing with many injustices. At the young age of 14, in December 1958, I was traumatized after seeing the horrifying event happening right before my eyes; the Ku Klux Klan burned a cross in our yard one night. The perpetrators were never found.

Sadly, later that year our home was burned down from defective electrical wiring. My sister's two children were in the home at the time of the fire and died from this horrible accident. For years, my siblings who survived the fire and I were unable to discuss the tragic loss of our family members and home. This caused silent frustration in our family, and I carried that loss for many years. I believe I placed my anger into playing baseball to try to forget that sad moment of my family's and my life, by applying my grief into developing my talents and skills in baseball.

As I was maturing into adulthood, I saw many people that I truly believe had the gift of a Warrior's Mentality. It was not by the words they spoke, but by their action. I don't mean to slight any other family member or any other warrior with a spiritual mindset, but I will start with three of my family members. An experience that I witnessed – the faith and strength of my three sisters, Pearl, Alice, and Margaret required a Warrior's Mentality. Each sister had a child who died a terrifying death: Evelyn and Bobby Lewis were burned to death in a house fire at the age of three, and Peter drowned at the age of ten; two toddlers and one pre-teen child. So, as I witnessed my sisters' faith and strength, knowing that the chain had been broken, but through faith it will be put back together again. (I Thessalonians 4:13-18).

In 1958, at the age of 13 to 14, something was in my spirit that I could not fully understand so I ignored it. As my teen years continued, I noticed that many of my classmates and others were asking me for advice and sometimes directions in certain situations in their lives. Since I was also a teenager, I thought it was strange for them to be asking me. Like others at that young age, I neither understood nor recognized that the spirit within me was God using His greatest works to prepare me to assist mankind (John 14:12).

I was dealing with situations at home. My brother, the oldest sibling of 14, was overtaken with a scenario that I did not think he could overcome. My friends and others thought I would be able to change the situation. If I had understood how to exercise the spirit within me, perhaps I could have. I do believe that recognizing the spirit was the beginning of what I would need in the future for a warrior's mentality. Unfortunately, as I just turned 17, I watched my brother pass away; not being able to help was horrifying and devastating.

Don't let anyone steal your dream. Just as Joseph, at 17, the 11th son of Jacob, was a dreamer (Genesis 37:5, 6), with a spirit that God had put in him at a young age, exercised his gift early, it got him into trouble and almost cost him his life. Of course, God had a plan for his life, and it was to save many lives. Anytime somebody tries to do you harm with the spirit living in you, God can turn it into good. (Genesis 50:20). As Joseph was a dreamer, so was I. When I was young, I would lie in bed daydreaming and thinking about the things I wished I could do to help my family, because my parents supported us on a sharecropper's salary. Before being trained and studying the word, I was vulnerable. I didn't know I needed to put on the helmet of salvation. Because spiritual battles begin in the mind, an area of critical spiritual conflict that leads to the heart, and controls your thoughts, behavior, and decisions, I didn't learn this life-saving truth until I was a young adult.

My early steps in faith began at the age of 11, with baptism at Weeping Mary Baptist Church in Bowling

Green, SC by Reverend Mack Moore. In that era, my parents thought that my being baptized was the right thing to do, even though I did not have a personal relationship with the Lord Jesus Christ. My parents continued to take me to church. I learned a lot by going to Sunday School and listening to the gospel being preached every Sunday morning. I learned more about Jesus Christ from my Aunt Elizabeth Caldwell McClure, who was also my powerful Sunday School teacher. I continued to mature in the faith and was a part of the Usher Ministry in the church.

Weeping Mary Baptist Church was the heart of our family's spiritual life. My dad and two of my uncles were deacons. They were faithful, hardworking men. They were sharecroppers, farmers, and took care of their families. At the age of 14, I saw these God-fearing men come to a sigh of weariness. Our beloved church burned to the ground; we were forced to hold church in a tent for a year. The church was originally built in 1914, rebuilt in 1954, and went up in flames in 1960. The men and women put their faith into action by biblical precepts. (James 2:17-20) "And by prayer and faith in our Lord Jesus Christ." They put nickels and dimes together; with the sacrifices of the members, the new church building was built in 1961.

The church prospered holistically for decades under Holy Spirit-filled ministers of the gospel. As I look back, I am proud to know that I was baptized there, and my faith journey began as a faithful worker in the Usher's Ministry and as a dedicated Sunday School member. I was blessed to attend many revival services and listen to anointed preachers of the gospel. The Word of God touched my spirit and ignited me to study the Scriptures with a passion. I look back today to those times and having the gift of teaching. I realize that hearing the Gospel preached repeatedly made me "diligent to present myself to God without being ashamed of rightly dividing the word of truth." (2 Timothy 2:15)

In the past, I was in between two types of mentalities: Fixed and Growth. I was in the Fixed Mentality for many years because of the oppression I was under in that era, 62 years ago. I never thought that I would have the ability to change. When I was of middle school age through high school, I was trying just to survive. I had not been taught about the growth mindset. All I knew during that time was the stone, unchangeable fixed mentality. I did not realize I could be a free, victorious warrior. As I matured in life, I learned about Growth Mentality when I received the gift of discernment (I Corinthians 12:10).

I knew, with my ability and talents, God could further develop my skills. As I embraced the growth mentality, my mental and physical mindsets were enhanced. I was blessed to launch a successful baseball career.

My motivation to play baseball at an early age was influenced by my dad, who was born at the turn of the century as a "sharecropper". He did not have the opportunity to get a formal education, and therefore could neither read nor write, except for family endeavors. My father and mother had 14 children. My brothers and I, in the early 1950's began to play (organized sports) baseball and basketball. I fell deeply in love with playing ball and played at an early age. It helped to take my mind off things we didn't have.

A fan said I remember hearing people talking

about a baseball team in our small town and the team players' names sounding familiar. As a young person, I began to investigate to see what it was all about. After investigating and seeing some of the faces of players on the team, I discovered that some of them were my relatives. I began to go to the baseball games they played on the baseball field behind Roosevelt School. This was a time of excitement and joy for me, as well as many other citizens in the community. We looked forward each week to go to the games. These games had a big impact on my life, as well as other fans in this town, especially young people.

There were no other activities in the small community in the summer after the school year, especially for African Americans. Yes, there was a beautiful swimming pool, and other recreational things in this town, but they were on the east side of town. Caucasian families lived there; and we were prohibited from using the pool and participating in all the activities.

A fan said we looked forward to going to the baseball games on Saturdays and Sundays and enjoyed watching the games that the Hornets played. Looking back, I realize that those games helped to keep me and many young people my age and older from the abuse of alcohol, marijuana, and other addictive drugs at that time. We chose to watch and observe how the Hornet players conducted themselves on and off the field. Some of them were married, had families, and conducted themselves in a respectable manner; what a great example for me and the other young men in this community. We watched those Hornets players become great family men and honorable citizens in the respective communities. Thank you, Hornets Team, for having a positive impact on me… and this Community!!!

In 1958, when I was 14, there was a field behind our church in Bowling Green, South Carolina. The men of the church converted it into a nice baseball field with a pitcher's mound, infield and a huge outfield. That was my first real feeling of playing baseball. I was able to develop my skills for playing different positions and learned about competition and respect for opponents while having the desire to "win". Those days gave me the discipline to improve and better my skills to try out for the high school team. I made the varsity team with the Roosevelt High School baseball team in Clover, South Carolina at the age of sixteen.

Being a sharecropper's son, we couldn't afford transportation. This limitation resurfaced when I was scheduled to play in Gastonia for the Pittsburgh Pirates. In the late 50's, early 60's, I did not have a ride or a way to get to the Tryouts. It was miles away. It resonated with me for many years with regret and sorrow that I couldn't try out for the Pittsburgh Pirates.

After spending some time in Brooklyn, New York, I observed several Semi-Pro teams; this inspired me to improve my skills and made me more dedicated than ever to this game. Having lived through these times helped teach me patience; it led me to follow in God's word to help people realize we are all the same on the inside. I came back to the Carolinas in 1964 and began to play Semi-Pro baseball.

The most rewarding of all my achievements was getting married (Proverbs 18:22) and being blessed with children, grandchildren and great-grandchildren. It was fate that I met my wife, Jymmie Jackson. She visited Weeping Mary Baptist Church with her classmate, Ellie Rollinson Barnett, one Sunday morning. I don't recall if I was ushering that Sunday. My future wife asked who I was, and her friend stated, "You don't want to meet him because he is too young." We are the same age. One day she came to Roosevelt High School to visit and peeked into my classroom window. The rest is history.

My wife, Jymmie Jackson McClure, was a life member of Tabernacle Baptist Church. I began dating Jymmie and attending church with her in 1960 and would visit her church until 1964 when I joined. I graduated from high school in 1962, and we were married at an early age. I was nurtured and matured in the faith under some dynamic pastors and deacons. Along with a renewed warrior mindset, I learned how to get along with mankind. (Romans 12:18)

In the early 1960's, during my baseball career, our teams were segregated. We knew deep down in our spirit that to be successful, we must be color blind. The new mindset became contagious throughout our teams. Hundreds of players in the Negro League started to exemplify what it means to have this new mindset and to see past color on the team. We would go out and recruit Caucasians and other ethnic groups to be on our teams. During that era, we were the first team to integrate in the entire county. I was honored that our team historian, Lewis Burris, reported it to a sportswriter from the Enquirer Herald of York County, South Carolina. Lewis recounted that I was instrumental in integrating our baseball team, and I did so by introducing several white players to our team. One of those players, among many, was Terry Thomas. Terry was a great all-around player. One of the greatest moments of his career, and a great joy for me, was to see him hit a home run over the "green monster" wall of the Boston Red Sox farm club park in Winston-Salem, North Carolina. One of the greatest accomplishments in my sports career was to have a part in integrating the first local baseball team in York County, South Carolina.

I finished my career with a multitude of home runs and RBIs and tied at second place. In 1984, I retired from playing baseball. After all that I accomplished in this great sport, it was still not my greatest accomplishment….

This wouldn't have happened with a fixed mindset. I now had a warrior mindset as well as the mind of Christ (Philippians 2:5) that gave me the ability to endure the trials, difficulties, and injustices that I faced in the late 1950s and 60s. As I continued to mature with my new mindset as a warrior, I knew it was not Earthly success. It was the spiritual achievement through faith by embracing the words of Philippians 4:13, "I can do all things through Christ who strengthens me."

Injustices

The year was 1959. It was still during the Jim Crow era. Blacks were still treated unfairly. I clearly remember a time my nephew Charles and I had the opportunity to work for a rich, white man, plowing his field with mules. The hourly wage was one dollar an hour. However, at the end of the week, we were paid only five dollars. He paid us one dollar per day, knowing that we should have received one dollar an hour for our work. As I studied African American history, I saw that the slave masters counted our ancestors as three-fifths of a person. We felt the effects of it because they thought they were superior, and we were inferior. Therefore, my faith was challenged again and again. I put my faith in Christ Jesus, as I heard Him say, "Come to me all you who labor and are heavy laden, and I will give you rest." (Matthew 11:28-30).

Having witnessed the Ku Klux Klan burning a cross in the middle of the night on the front lawn of my home, caused me to go through a dilemma. Martin Luther King, Jr. advocated for non-violent demonstrations, and my parents had always told me to "always do the right thing." However, being a young African American adult male, when the Ku Klux Klan burned that cross in my front yard just because of the color of our skin, made it difficult.

Civil Rights leader Malcolm X said, "We are nonviolent with people who are non-violent with us." I am for the truth, no matter who tells it; I am for justice no matter who it is for. Again, we declare our rights to be human beings; to be given respect as a human, to be given the rights of a human being in this society.

While in middle school, I recall hearing about an African American male high school freshman named Emmett Till who was kidnapped at 2:30 a.m. He was found shot in the head, beaten to death, and tied with barbed wire on a mill fan. He was thrown into the Tallahatchie River in Mississippi. All that was done at the hands of two white men. It was stated the reason for the killing was that he whistled and flirted with a white woman. One of the men, who was later acquitted for the murder was the husband of the white woman. The images of the disfigured face of Emmett Till burned in my underdeveloped mind, and at the same time I had been told that African Americans were 3/5th of human beings. This was demonstrated by not allowing us to have voting rights, quality education, equal employment or decent housing. How was I to overcome this with a fixed mindset? This prompted me to do what was necessary to achieve equal rights. I remain committed to self-education on matters of equity and human rights, and I have actively participated in demonstrations to support and advance the cause of equality.

Baseball Career

My baseball career became both an escape and a rebellion. I studied the game of baseball. In 1884, the first black man to play Major League baseball, years before Jackie Robinson was a player, was a player named Moses Fleetwood Walker. Growing up, we heard a lot of talk about The Negro League (1920-1950) and all the great players that were not permitted in the Major League. This gave the players the drive to go into the Major Leagues. When I returned to the Carolinas, the first team I played with was the Gastonia Blue Socks. The team was organized by Raymond Hill. It was then that I met his youngest son, Elmore Hill. Elmore and I played for the Blue Socks, and I spent a lot of time mentoring him into a fine baseball player. Elmore once stated, "I was so proud to see him develop into one of the best ball players Gaston County had seen." My mentoring and instruction to Moe in his earlier years influenced his very successful career.

The second team I played with was The State Line Sluggers. This was a team which had players on both sides of the state line (North and South Carolina). It was one of the best teams in the Carolinas. There were twins on the team, named James and John Thomas. They were two of the best duos that I had ever seen playing baseball and I had the pleasure of playing on the team with them. They were such skilled baseball players that they were scouted by the Minnesota Twins. The Minnesota Twins did not want them only for a mascot for the Twin City, but because they were truly skilled baseball players. The Minnesota Twins sent them to go to the minor-league team for a short period of time before entering the major leagues; but there was a big problem. The twins were only 17 years old, nearly 18, and they needed their parents to sign for them to go play. Their parents wouldn't sign for them to go because they thought the boys would be treated unfairly because of the color of their skin during the Jim Crow era. This was such a great opportunity that was missed. This did not stop James and John from going on to become the best semi-pro duo baseball players that I believe were on the planet. They finished a remarkable career with multiple home runs and RBIs and close to a

600 slugging percent and career averages of 300 plus. My wife Jymmie and I traveled to and lived in Brooklyn, New York where I was able to observe some dynamic semi pro baseball clubs. This motivated me to pursue a baseball career.

Prejudice in New York was not as blatant as it was in the South. During this time when we were living in New York we went back to North Carolina, my wife was pregnant with our first child. We went downtown to find an obstetrician to care for her during her pregnancy. We had never been as humiliated as we were after we walked into the doctor's office and were quickly told to leave because their office was for whites only!

In the early 1960s, I had a job working at an orthopedic hospital, making less than the minimum wage; it was a struggle to support my wife and child. The Civil Rights movement was in full swing at that time. I remember marching in my city to protest for equal rights. We fought for the right to vote, to go to movie theaters and restaurants, and the right to equal education in a decent school system. We wanted to be treated like human beings and treated with the same respect as others. We were asked to march peacefully. With an abundance of injustices still happening, it was a difficult choice.

I knew of no integrated baseball teams in York County, South Carolina, prior to the 1960s and early 70s. The legal system was stacked against black citizens for about 100 years, 1865 – 1968. Jim Crow Laws were a collection of state and local statutes that legalized racial segregation. The purpose of Jim Crow laws was to reestablish white supremacy and codified the segregation of whites and blacks. Some Jim Crow rules made it unlawful for any amateur white baseball team to play baseball on any vacant lot or baseball diamond within two blocks of a playground devoted to the Negro race; it was unlawful for any amateur colored baseball team to play baseball in any vacant lot or baseball diamond within two blocks of any playground devoted to the white race. (Georgia Jim Crow laws)

Some Other Jim Crow Laws That Were Legalized.

1. Never assert or intimate that a white person is lying.
2. Never impute dishonorable intentions to a white person.

3. Never suggest that a white person ever is from an inferior class.
4. Never lay claim to or overly demonstrate superior knowledge or intelligence above a white person.
5. Never use profanity or curse at a white person.
6. Never laugh derisively at a white person.
7. Never comment on the appearance of a white female.

(Stetson Kennedy, the author of Jim Crow Guide (1990)

As I got older and matured. I began to march in demonstrations to be treated fairly. I remember marching alongside my friend and coworker Clinzo Meeks down Main Street in Gastonia, NC while thousands of Caucasians on the sidewalks and tops of buildings were calling us the N-word, yelling to us, "Monkeys, go back to Africa!" This and other racial slurs were shouted at us throughout our entire march. It was a dilemma for me to be non-violent, or violent.

As you could imagine, it was traumatizing for youngsters and adults during those times, especially not having the growth mentality of a Victorious Warrior.

I have been transformed by the power of the Holy Spirit (II Corinthians 3:18) and filled with the Holy Spirit (Acts 1:8). This was a continuation and confirmation of my victory with a warrior mentality. My healing and forgiveness process began with Matthew 6:15 and that's what Jesus said, "It is all about forgiveness."

After I was forgiven for the anger and bitterness that was in my heart, I was set free (John 8:36; Galatians 5:1). Without a doubt, knowing that success is color blind (Galatians 3:28), and having the spirit of a Victorious Warrior, I am to carry the good news around the world.

First, I was led to teach the Good News (Matthew 28:19-20; II Timothy 2:2), and by being obedient, I was blessed to teach and mentor students from preschool, middle school, high school, and freshmen. Looking back, that was the fulfilling part of being and having a warrior's mentality. The rewarding aspect of it is when those students come back and tell me that I made a positive impact on their lives.
I have been teaching the Word of God in the church and community for over 40 years and have been very blessed

in both locations. There have been many students encouraging me by just saying that I have been blessed by the Word, often not knowing I had demonic forces trying to lead me astray from my community. Some of my Saturday morning Bible study students such as my wife, Jymmie McClure; sister, Doris Williams; and church members, Phyllis Whitworth and Joyce Hoyle, whose words of encouragement kept echoing in my spirit to help keep me on the right path. To God be the glory! (Proverbs 4:25-27) I am still blessed with the ability to be teaching to this day.

The amazing fact that something positive began to take place in plain sight. These young students that were being tutored at the peak of integration are the students that said I made an impression. They said it gave them confidence to look back and see how a great number of African Americans, Caucasians and other ethnic groups have come together and are successful.

It reminds me of what I communicated, as it was communicated to me, that God has given everyone a fingerprint that is different from anyone else's. Therefore, we can leave an imprint that no one else can.

As I look back and see the success of the groups of people working together, it truly shows that success is colorblind. (Galatians 3:28) There is neither Jew nor Greek; there is neither slave nor free; there is neither male nor female; for you are all one in Christ Jesus. In Christ all racial barriers to salvation are abolished, there is neither Jews nor Greeks in Christ. All social barriers to salvation are abolished, there is neither slave nor free. All gender barriers to salvation are abolished for there's neither male or female (Colossians 3:10-11) Every believers has equal standing before God. Therefore, success is colorblind because all have been successfully set free. I believe this confirms that one of the real ingredients of success in how to get along with others. Success is not about what material things you have acquired or about how much academic knowledge you have, but it is to love your neighbor as yourself. (Matthew 22:39)

Baseball ultimately crowned my warrior's journey. Playing again in my hometown, where I started my career, turned out to be the best move that I made in baseball.

I also had the great honor of playing with the Bowling Green Hornets Semi Pro Baseball Team where I first began to play baseball, on the field behind the church.

In my career with the Bowling Green Hornets, we set records in baseball, including winning the 1973 Cross-County Baseball Championship. I was selected to play with the All-Star team. Having a batting average of 400 plus, I finished with a great career. I had a multitude of Home Runs and RBIs. I finished second place for Home Runs and RBIs with Bobby Kennedy.

Ed Pressley was the leading Home Run and RBI hitter. The Hornets sought out the best talent in players. I recruited young players without regard to their race, and the Hornets were the first integrated team near here at the time, thus "winning with the "Best". This was mentioned in the "Enquirer" newspaper article written by Jamie Self in 2010.

Bobby Kennedy stated that I was his mentor and helped to guide him in the early part of his career. He had the experience of seeing me, his mentor, making the first triple play in baseball. Bobby Kennedy finished with a great career and multiple Home "Runs and RBIs". Also John Davis, a pitcher on our team was one the winningness pitcher in The League, and Sammie Lipcomb was a great speeder and finished with a great career.

David Robbin, a great teammate, displayed a great faith to our team and community when an horrific incident occurred that devasted his family and community.

James Robert Adams "Chino" was the President of the baseball club and very inspirational to the team's success. He made sure that all the dynamics were just right on the playing fields before every game. He had one of the strongest throwing arms in the league.

Lewis Burris was one of the senior members on the team; he was a great catcher, and the greatest in giving directions on how to position players in the game. He was the only switch hitter on the team and finished with a great career. Lewis also was the team treasurer and secretary. He did an outstanding job all the way around.

Larry Burris was a pitcher and threw a 4-hitter in the

Championship game.

The first time our team met an opponent, we defeated them 99.9% of the time! We faced such powerful teams as the Lancaster Tigers. When we met this team, they had not been beaten in five straight years. The other team was owned and managed by my mentor, Nelson A. Petree. Nelson was the owner of a semi-pro baseball team called The Pond Giants. He encouraged me in my career. I admired how skillfully Mr. Petree managed his team, how he mentored me, and helped to navigate many players to go play Pro baseball.

Nelson Petree's semi pro baseball team was allowed to have the home field of the minor league Farm Club of the Boston Red Sox for their home field. I had the pleasure and honor to be on a team that won the Tri-Country Cross County Baseball Championship. There were many super athletes in that championship game. I was blessed to drive a 365-foot home run out of the park. In the series, I was the leading hitter with seven hits. In the same year, I was selected to play in the Charlotte-Mecklenburg Cross County All-Star game with a batting average of 400 plus.

During my career, I was able to meet great baseball stars such as Bobby Richardson who played with the New York Yankees, alongside Mickey Mantle. Bobby was an eight-time all-star. He won the Gold Glove five consecutive times playing second base. I had the honor of being with Bobby Richardson during the Hall of Fame Induction of my mentor, Nelson Petree.

My greatest legacy emerged through those I mentored. I spent a lot of time mentoring Elmore Hill who was developed into a fine baseball player. Elmore signed with the Baltimore Orioles at the age of 17. He later played with the Minnesota Twins for five years. He accomplished great things during his baseball career.

As a Midwest League player, Elmore played in 969 games, hitting 201 home runs and 720 RBIs during his career. He went on to become one of the best hitting instructors. I was proud to hear him say that I, along with others such as Ed and Dick Pressley, encouraged him in his career. Willie Gillispise, along with Elmore Hill, were the first African Americans to play Post Legion Baseball in the state of North Carolina. They had to deal with racial injustices because during this time, people had prejudices about these two African Americans playing alongside them on the baseball field. Willie was 15 years old in 1964 when asked to play his first Post Legion baseball game. In 1966, Willie Gillispise led Gastonia with a .419 batting average. Bobby Kennedy was the third player I had the pleasure of mentoring. He saw me make the first triple play in baseball. He played alongside me on the Bowling Green Hornets baseball team. He finished his career with multiple home runs and RBIs.

I have a message to any upcoming baseball players, "What lies ahead will always be a mystery so don't be afraid to explore!" I have a message for everybody to ponder that I was not fully aware of until I was transformed into victory with a warrior mentality while being set free (Romans 12:2). Physically we are children of men. But spiritually, we are children of God.

Whoever lives in love, lives in God (I John 4:16). Two foundational aspects of God's character are love and light, and man is meant to exhibit these qualities. (Matthew 5:14) The account of the creation reveals an interesting fact that we often overlook today. God didn't create man for heaven. He created man for Earth. God is the ruler of heaven, and He made man to express His authority on earth; God wants him to share His rule. Therefore, we must have a victorious mentality mindset to obey God's authority and have the manifold wisdom of God.

With the mentality mindset that's been given to me by the Spirit of God, (I Corinthians 12:10) God will allow me to know a person who is full of love; He doesn't do anything for His purpose alone. A selfish person wants all the glory, all the credit, all the recognition, all the attention, all the power, all the authority, all the rights, and all the privileges. This is an individual that is not transformed with a new mindset.

Knowledge acquires facts and recites God's truth; Wisdom knows when and how to apply God's truth to a specific situation. It is truly stated that: People that value their privileges above their principles soon lose both. We must never forget that all our strength comes from God, not the number of people that gather in our assemblies. I think it's been biblically proven that sometimes the lesser amount of people, the greater the anointing, for example, (Judges 7:1-9). Gideon defeated an army of thousands of men with only 300 men providing proof that the victory of a warriors' mentality was not due to the number of men with him, but by divine intervention. (Matthew 18:15-20). Just as Jesus spoke about a dispute with a brother, He emphasized the anointing power on the small amount of two or three gatherings.

True, men and women were always to be victorious warriors for Christ. God didn't create man only to be a servant but to be a son who is involved in taking care of the things in the Earthly realm. (Genesis 1:27-28) This means that God doesn't want man to work for Him. (2 Corinthians 6:1 NLT). Before I was transformed with a new mindset, I would say I am working for Jesus, but then I realized if I was working for Jesus as a hired hand, it was instead of being a partner and a joint heir. (Romans 8:17) When I pondered on the implications of being a son of God's and being joint heir with Christ, it really refreshed my new mindset; it empowered and increased my faith with a knowledge to know that I should not worry about my day-to-day living expenses, such as where I will get food to eat, water to drink, or clothes to wear. Now, more than ever before, I understand what my father meant when He said, "Ask, seek, knock." (Matthew 6:31-34) My friends and brothers in God's plan, you see there's always plenty of provision to go around (Philippians 4:19).

Now I must know my purpose; God has equipped me (mankind) to carry out the purpose and function He has given me. You can make many plans, but the Lord's purpose will prevail. (Proverbs 19:21) When I married at the age of 17, I had no clue of the purpose of man, not knowing then that the male is the foundation of the human family. Along the way, some ethnic group thought and, in some instances, treated me as though I was a lesser human being. Deep inside my spirit I knew it was not the purpose that God had for my family.

When a negative history predicts your future, your present is in trouble. But my friend, when you get the knowledge of the purpose and calling of the Creator of the universe for your life, that you were chosen before the foundation of the world, it sets you free. (Ephesians 1:4,5) We should know God's purpose and what He has qualified for us. Ask for it because the story of the prodigal son is a case in point (Luke 15:11-32). The son demanded from his father what was coming to him. If you do not know your purpose in life, it can be disastrous. My question to you is, "Can you handle what you ask for?" Assignment means a task or something that has been entrusted to us to do. Our assignment determines a person's purpose.

The responsibilities with which God has entrusted us are very clear and they indicate His purpose (Genesis 2:15-16). It is important for the male to know that God's purpose was and is for the male to be the visionary leader of the family. This doesn't mean that women don't also have the capacity to be visionaries and leaders. However, the male is the one to whom God first entrusted His plans and purposes.

Thanks be to God; I learned the purpose in life that God has for me. It's still an ever-learning work in process, (Proverbs 18:15). After maturing in the faith and God revealing my purpose, I look back and remember my high school days and graduating. I did not finish at the top of my class. Several of my classmates finished with a 4.0 academic achievement; some 3.0, and I finished with

2.0, just a C average. Decades after school, I wrote my first book. One of my classmates who finished with a high GPA, communicated that out of ALL of our classmates, he never thought I would be the one to write a book. Maybe he failed to realize that nothing is impossible with God (Luke 1:37).

Again, I have released the anger, resentment, and bitterness that I had been carrying around and thought I was entitled to because some ethnic groups thought they had been given the green light and were superior, while others and I were inferior. Just as my classmate thought I was the least likely to write a book, they failed to realize that I had been transformed with a new mindset of love and forgiveness. Once God began to show me my purpose and life goals, I realized the most skillful or gifted person does not always win – sometimes the outcome involves timing and opportunity (Ecclesiastes 9:11).

Forgiveness !

I observed how two amazing people demonstrated forgiveness, Cornelia Arnolda Johanna "Corrie" ten Boom and Nelson Mandela. Corrie ten Boom is renowned for her bravery and faith during the Holocaust. She's known for her stories about forgiveness. Corrie ten Boom delivers a message of forgiveness to a former guard who had persecuted her during the Holocaust. It is a powerful testament to the liberating nature of forgiveness even after suffering unimaginable horrors. Corrie chose not to be consumed by hatred. This allowed her to live a life of peace and service to humanity. She was an advocate for forgiveness and reconciliation. She even extended it to those who persecuted her during the Holocaust.

One of her famous quotes, "Every experience God gives us, every person He puts in our lives, is perfect preparation for the future that only He can see." Corrie ten Boom highlights in her writings about the liberations she gets from her forgiveness to others. After all the challenging circumstances she has encountered, she still displays love.

Nelson Mandela spent 27 years in prison, mainly for his activism against South Africa's apartheid. Nelson Mandela then became president of South Africa; a proven fact that success is colorblind. He asked some of his security team to go have lunch with him at a restaurant in the city. As they sat down and ordered their food, Mandela noticed someone sitting in front of his table waiting for food. He told a member of the security team to ask that person to eat with them. The man obliged. He brought his food and sat by Mandela. The man's hands were trembling constantly until everyone had finished eating. Once everyone finished, the man went on his way. The security team noticed and thought the man was apparently quite sick as his hands trembled as he ate.

"No, not at all," Mandela said. "This man was a prison guard where I was imprisoned. After the torture I was subjected to, I would scream and ask for water. The same man would come each time and urinate on my head. I find him to be scared and trembling, expecting me to retaliate in the same way by torturing or imprisoning him now that I am the president of South Africa." It was not in Nelson Mandela's character nor part of his ethics to retaliate in that manner. This is total forgiveness. "The mentality of retaliation destroys states," "The mentality of tolerance builds nations."

I have seen just how merciful, gracious and forgiving God is. If humans such as Corrie ten Boom and Nelson Mandela can have forgiveness, surely, I can have forgiveness for those that have mistreated my family and me, especially in the early 1950s, 1960s, and BEYOND. Remember that hate is too great a burden to bear, it injures hater more than the hated. Decades later, my faith faced a new test. During the mid-2000's, I was saddened to learn of some ungodly news about my beloved church, Weeping Mary Baptist Church, the church in which my sister was still a life member. The allegations were investigated; the evidence was in writing; and yet it was denied by the current leadership. This broke my heart as it led to a large lawsuit against the church.

Three ladies who were aged 74, 80 and 81 had been members of the church their entire lives and were the only members of the entire church body to stand boldly for the truth and against denunciation of a member for false accusations. In telling the truth, these three saints were voted out of the church without following biblical principles. (Matthew 18:15-17).

Although one of these saints was my sister, it did not stop her, nor the others' faith walk (2 Corinthians 5:7). "Trust in the Holy Scriptures, God will bring every word into judgment including every secret thing whether good or evil" (Ecclesiastes 12:13-14). "And there is no creature hidden from His sight, but all things are naked and open to the eyes of Him to whom we must give account" (Hebrews 4:13).

Preserving our history orally and in written form is important. Unfortunately, a lot of church history was lost during the early-2000s when we had a Clean-Up Day at church. Some important documents were thrown away without realizing how valuable they were: items such as ledger books, the documents to negotiate the buying of property at the current church location which occurred in 1977, baptism records, and other legal documents of importance were lost.

A vital opportunity that was missed for so many years was the opportunity for church historian to interview my wife's mother, Deaconess Juanita Jackson, who was the oldest member of Tabernacle Baptist Church in Gastonia, NC until her death in January 2021, at the age of 97. Born in 1923, she saw the church's early days and could have provided valuable insights and historical context. Her absence serves as a poignant reminder of the importance of capturing and preserving our history, while we still have the chance. As Sister Jackson's mother told her in 1926, at just three years old, Tabernacle Baptist Church was born. I sat at Mrs. Jackson's feet and listened in awe to the history of the church as she told us her memories of the things her mother and father shared with her. Sister Jackson shared her knowledge of the church starting when she was in her early adolescent years. My time spent listening to her story covered 97 years of history of the church. There was one thing she would always tell me, and she would always say my name when she said, "Frank, take one day at a time." That is something I try to remember every day.

Her parents, Cora and Wilson Caldwell, would tell her how they would sell hotdogs, chicken, and fish dinners to help pay the bills and upkeep of Queen Hall on Bradley Street in Gastonia, NC, then the new location on North York Street. Fifteen states in the United States passed wage laws for white people to make 0.16/hour and African Americans to make 0.10/hour. This was the reason why our church and many other churches at that time had to sell items to pay the church bills. As the church moved forward, they taught and enlightened everyone on the biblical way of giving and receiving. The founding members learned as we do now to give from our hearts (II Corinthians 9:6-9).

As I matured in Christ, I was under the leadership of approximately six pastors that helped navigate me through my spiritual journey of Faith in the Lord Jesus Christ. The six pastors have been the Reverends: Mack Moore, Jackson Jones, Paul Barnett, Jason Scott, Vernon Worthy and currently Pastor Dr. Benjamin Hinton. The one that I matured the most in faith was under Pastor Vernon Worthy. My faith was not where it should have been, but under Reverend Worthy's leadership I grew. As I grew and matured, the Lord led him to appoint and ordain me as a deacon along with John Dunlap in 1983 to be a servant of the body of Christ.

After witnessing those hurtful events at a really young age, and as I advanced in years and embracing Faith, there was still a void in my life. I tried many avenues to fill that void; one avenue was Masonry. I joined a Masonic lodge, and over time I eventually received 32 degrees. Over time, that did not fill the spiritual void in my life I was seeking. Masonry did teach me a great lesson on brotherhood; how to treat and greet each other, as well as humanity, on a godly level with no hidden agenda. Communicate (Romans 12:18) "If it is possible, as far as depends on you, live peacefully with all mankind." If you live that way, you will meet on the level and part on the square with honesty, integrity, and mutual respect. This implies that all dealings have been fair and above board, and all are satisfied with the interaction.

This taught me that all individuals are equal and treated with respect when they meet, regardless of social standing or background. This Organization (Brance) shows so much Love, and emphasizes Honesty, Integrity and Respect. Therefore, I observe the quotation: "When an honest man discovers he is mistaken, he will either cease being mistaken or cease being honest!" I've learned from that - if I make an error, I will correct it; but if I refuse to do so, I will lose my Honesty. As I earlier wrote, my heart desires to see everyone work toward being on a godly level. I think a great place to start is in the community because church and other organizations are birthed by the community, and I believe in educating and empowering the communities.

Therefore, I have dedicated my time and gifts to community, because I believe that Americans, especially in ranking positions, are becoming anti-social, a behavior that involves actions that disregard the rights of others and disrupt social order. Studies show that communities that have meetings open to everyone, to discuss community issues and problems, promote better neighborhoods, new friendships, compromise and interactions that can boost fewer drug addictions, longer lifespan, lower suicide rates, and more happiness. Those communities that don't meet and interact, as described above, have the reverse of the positive benefits listed above. People were meant to interact; to work and produce together. (Isaiah 1:18) Not doing this is overlooking a basic human requirement. I believe it is the reason that people today are more divided than ever. (Matthew 12:25). I think that every community should have a "Confidentiality" individual that a family can trust; one of the most difficult issues for a family in the community to deal with, or talk with family concerning, is suicide. I have first-hand experience – to be with dear, close friends when they got the news that one of their two children had committed suicide.

Their father and I had gone to the same school when we were younger and graduated from there to pursue our careers. We both were blessed to be selected to play semi-pro baseball, and to travel to many cities. After retiring from baseball, we both pursued a challenging bowling career. We participated and competed in tournaments across the southeast, with our spouses, traveling by bus, with three or four teams. We were closely knitted together just as a community. As we traveled home from one of our trips, my friend and our spouses were informed that one of his sons had committed suicide. It was devastating for his family, our teams, and the community. The father and mother were strong in their faith, and we, as teams and the community, stood by them in that challenging time. As I stated earlier, it would help to have a counselor, educated in suicide prevention, who could communicate how to prevent suicide and the signs of it.

Maybe if our community had been educated on at least one or all five of these preventatives, it may have prevented the loss of life for our friend's son. I learned the main reasons that people take their own life, including depression, are mental conditions that lead to disorder by disconnecting from reality. This can be caused by environmental stressors, substance use, and other events or conditions that act as triggers.

Mental health conditions that lead to impulsive thoughts, feeling like there is no other option, allow their thoughts the use of a method to take their life; and some terminate their life because of terminal illness. I am reminding my readers and others to please be aware of the many reasons and help to save a life. Bring peace to a family by educating them where to cast their anxiety, the suicide prevention telephone no# 988. (I Peter 5:7,8). Recognize. Respond. Refer. Remember, every person in all communities is your neighbor. (Matthew 22:39). We must show and emphasize action in our communities by being doers. (James 1:22). Over the years, I recognized that what was weak in me, magnified what was strong in God! (II Corinthians 12:9) "Blessing"

Despite the multiple things that my family and I were going through, our church family began to experience some difficult times. The chairman of our Deacon ministry, Deacon Ed McMillan's health began to fail, and he was no longer able to lead the Deacon's ministry. I was asked to take on that role as leader of the Deacons' ministry, but I declined it repeatedly, asking the deacons, "Why me?" They insisted that I would be a good fit, especially Deacon Ed Dunlap, among the other deacons.

I went into serious prayer because I knew that my God would give me the answer. After praying about it, He allowed me to see the strong, Holy Spirit-filled deacons' shoulders that I could stand on with the guidance of the Holy Spirit. Some of those God-fearing men were Deacons Ed McMillan, Thomas Garvin, Ed Dunlap,

James Jackson, Lyntallus Holland, Andrew Blair, Alex Guthrie and Earnest Garvin. It was a blessing to have the Holy Spirit working and these men's shoulders to stand on. Several years after I accepted the chairmanship, in 1989, our pastor at the time, Reverend Worthy, resigned. Therefore, I, along with the other deacons, had the responsibility of leading one of the largest congregations in the African American community. For nearly two years, we were without an undershepherd and had an interim pastor who lived two hours away and came only on Sunday mornings. Until then, the burden was on us, guided by the Holy Spirit, to lead our congregation.

During this time of growth and transition, there was a significant amount of administrative work that needed to be done. Pastor Worthy's wife was secretary. Unfortunately, when Pastor Worthy left the church, she followed, leaving us without a secretary for the church. Thanks to God our Father, the Holy Spirit led Sister Dorothy (Dot) Guthrie to us. She stepped up and did an astounding job managing all the administrative duties and ensuring that everything ran smoothly. Her dedication and efficiency were instrumental in keeping the church's operations organized.

Presently, Patricia Butler has taken on this crucial role, and she has been able to fill those shoes admirably, supporting order and keeping all the administrative work in check. Her efforts continue to support the church's mission and contribute to our community's strength.

After much prayer and reviewing many resumes, the Holy Spirit led us to call Pastor Benjamin Hinton to be the undershepherd of our congregation. He was installed in 1991 as pastor. As he pursued his education, he was blessed with an earned doctorate, and the congregation grew tremendously. This growth prompted us, under Dr. Hinton's leadership, to build a new facility to accommodate the expansion.

Thanks be to God, we had strong ministries in place prior to, and more established under Dr. Hinton's leadership. Our deacons wore many hats and have always been working deacons in our church family. For example, Deacons William Sims and John Dunlap served as bus drivers for our Sunday School department, teachers, and former superintendents, and Chris Diggs. Deacon Thomas Garvin also served as General Superintendent. Other deacons worked in many other ministries in our church family. Deacon McMillan was the hymn choir leader for many years. When he passed on, Deacon Terry Chisholm, along with Deacon Andrew Bivens, stepped right in to lead the hymn choir and presently continue to lead the hymn choir.

Having choir ministries in our church was very important. Deacon Terry Chisholm's wife, Mamie Chisholm, was the director of all the choir groups and made sure that everything was in order. Sister Mamie understood that overseeing the choirs required being filled with the Holy Spirit; thus, the reason she was the leader of our choir ministries. Many people today still talk about the excellent work she did. The anointed singing still rings in our ears from the choirs: mass, senior, youth, and the Men of Distinction. By having such excellent ministries in our church and strong, Holy Spirit-led deacons, the most important nucleus of our church was, is, and always will be the WORD OF GOD.

Thanks be to God; we had strong ministries in place prior to and more established under Dr. Hinton's leadership. One noted ministry that we had was the Prison Outreach Ministry organized by Rev. Wilfort Powell, Brother Jeff Burris, and Clem McMillan. They went out into the prisons and ministered to the men in prison and even brought these brothers to church when allowed to do so. Jeff Burris was also a very dedicated Sunday School member. As the church continued to grow, the Lord blessed me to work with two great Deacons: Willie Dunovant and Chris Diggs to serve as co-chairmen. They worked alongside me faithfully with grace and dignity. I have served in the Deacon ministry for 40+ years.

I was honored to serve as the youth superintendent at Tabernacle Baptist Church for over 30 years with an excellent team: Minister Dorothy Guthrie (she was an advisor and assisted with all our youth). Mrs. Ernestine Davis (pianist/director of music) and Deacon Ben Williams (assistant superintendent). The motto that I always used in our team was "Molding Children." Our team protected the youth in the name of Jesus with all we had. At one time, we had a multitude of excellent teachers in the department, including Trustee Shawn Thomas, who had an exceptional gift for young people. We also had Ronnie Fox, along with Christine Hankerson, people that parents entrusted with their children. Most of our youth went on to further their education and some have become present-day educators, doctors, dentists, attorneys and entrepreneurs, to name a few.

I was honored to share several meanings of Christian education with superintendents, teachers, and students. Christian education is about allowing Christ to be formed in you through the power of the Holy Spirit. We can work hard to memorize Bible information, but if we are only gaining head knowledge, our Christian education is lacking. I communicated to the staff and students that it is about the heart being transformed; this only happens through a spiritual formation of wanting to be like Christ, knowing how Christ would act, and then acting likewise. I communicated to the superintendents and teachers that they need to teach students more than just facts, but also how to listen to God and follow his voice. It's not so much about how many ministries you have listed; at the end of the day, it's about spiritual formation (Romans 8:29), to be conformed to the image of Christ. "When believers are under such pressure and in such pain that they cannot even verbalize their desires, the Holy Spirit himself intercedes with groaning mere words cannot express" (Romans 8:26).

Out of all the leadership positions I held in ministry, being selected as General Superintendent was the most significant. It was not just a title; it was a serious ministry. I understood what the job entailed. It was the molding stage for children; it also educated the adults. I was able to teach students, teachers, and ministry superintendents. They needed guidance because they often came to me with biblical questions. This challenged me "To study to show myself approved." (2 Timothy 2:15). This was one of the greatest joys in my spiritual journey.

Although my role as General superintendent only lasted for approximately five years, I count it as one of the most fulfilling things in my faith journey. I would have liked to continue in that role but because of complications, the Holy Spirit led me to resign.

On my faith Journey, I met three praying Holy Ghost-filled ladies, the late Mrs. Dollie "Ma Mae" Whitworth, and ministers Shirley Greenlee and Martha Partlow. Their powerful testimonies had an impact on many lives, just as the woman at the well had (John 4:39-41). I am proud to call them my spiritual sisters in Christ. Deaconess Alfreda Brooks, the Former Education Director, worked diligently to help educate our entire church family, especially the youth. She, along with others, orchestrated and took the youth to statewide conventions in which the youth competed in many church programs. Under her guidance, our youth were successful in contributions to the state convention. She was the director of Vacation Bible School which was held in the mornings while the church was located on York Street; there were many children who attended Vacation Bible School. Deaconess Alfreda Brooks gave out Easter speeches which children would practice and memorize. This showed her dedication to "training up a child…." (Proverbs 22:6).

One of the greatest endeavors was for a woman of the church to be honored with a "Woman of the Year" award presented by Deaconess Alfreda Brooks. In acknowledgement to our past Sunday School Secretaries: Sister Maggie Hardin, Sister Phyllis Whitworth, Sister Mitchell Williams, and our current Educational Director, Minister Tangela White Hinton.

The growth of the church prompted us, under Dr. Hinton's leadership, to start our V2V campaign. We needed a new facility to accommodate the growth. The persons who were instrumental in the planning for the new church structure included our Pastor; trustees: George Barnette, Ron Williams, Antonio Lee; and Mr. J.C. Nichols, architect, and member of Tabernacle Baptist Church. The members of the Deacon ministry, along with many other ministry leaders, church members and community supporters played a role in the vision coming to fruition. God said to write the vision and make it plain. (Habakkuk 2:2). Going forward, by the leadership of our pastor, Dr. Benjamin Hinton, deacons, and trustees, the Lord blessed us to move into our new facility.

After a period in the new facility, I was led to take a sabbatical by the guidance of the Holy Spirit and the Word of God. In the press of time, the Holy Spirit as well as the Scripture revealed to me something that I was unable to see at the time. I found myself trying to understand this Scripture for a while and felt I was not coming to an understanding. I was baffled by I John 5:16. For me to fully grasp the meaning of these verses, God led me to the book of James 1:5 and Luke 13:9. During the time of the sabbatical, many things were revealed to me that came to fruition.

Many of my brothers and sisters did not understand; it was not properly communicated to the Body of Christ as to why I needed to take this sabbatical. It was a time where the Spirit had to nurture me and give me insight to understand what the Word of God was saying.

Worship

Being a leader and teacher of the Gospel for many years, I am asked many questions concerning the Gospel. The primary one is worship; according to the book of John 4:23,24, Jesus explained to the woman at the well, saying, "Yet a time is coming and has now come when the true worshipers will worship the Father in spirit and truth, for they are the kind of worshipers the Father seeks. God is spirit, and his worshipers must worship in spirit and in truth." I believe Jesus is saying that the way to worship Him is to have a pure heart, and unadulterated mind. God wants our worship toward him to be pure, not a performance, for the Father seeks such to worship him. It's an expression of honesty between our hearts and God's. God's example is David, a man after God's own heart (Acts 13:22). Some are so used to performing and trying to impress the people we want to love us, that we treat God the same way. Many try to make God happy without stopping to consider maybe what God wants from us, is nothing but us. We are kingdom children, and to be a kingdom child is to have a spiritual rule over the heart and lives of those who willingly submit to God's authority. (Luke 17:20-21; Romans 14:17).

Assembly Conversion/Tradition

One may ask why I talk about the Scripture so much in this book; just stop and think of the many people who won't read the Holy Scripture, but they will read a book or a novel. Many prayers in this book with Scripture in it will lead to conversion. (Romans 10:9). We need change of hearts (conversion) in all our government, in fact in every nation. You may ask why I can say this; just remember, it is written, "A tree is known by its fruit." (Matthew 12:13). We must try to reach all lost humanity. No matter where - be it in a book, in the community, or at the mall; sometimes a good evangelistic field can be in the pew where you may be sitting in a congregation. Don't assume everybody knows what you know; many people have an improper or unbiblical understanding of church attendance that borders on legalism. (excess moral law rather than religious faith) They are not aware that they feel they must attend every time there is any kind of service or meeting, or they risk God's wrath; some people experience guilt feelings whenever they miss for any reason.

Sadly, some assemblies encourage this kind of guilt; on the other hand, willful avoidance of assembly may indicate a problem in one's spiritual health. It is important to understand (Proverbs 4:7) that the quality of a person's relationship with God is not determined by how often he or she is in church; God's love for his children is not based on the number of times they attend formal services. There is no doubt that Christian followers of Jesus Christ should attend church. It should be the desire of every Christian to worship corporately, to fellowship with and encourage other Christians, (Ephesians 5:19; Colossians 3:16), not to come together in competition to see who can sing better, or who gives the most money! It should be about melody in our hearts to the Lord and giving thanks to God! (1 Thessalonians 5:11; 2 Timothy 3:16-17). This is for every Christian who proclaims the Word of God! A list of appropriate reasons for missing church is impossible to make. Only God knows the circumstances.

Of course, stay home when one is ill, but in other areas the issue comes down to your attitude and motivation (Think, Feel, Action, Willingness, Your Desire). A good reason for missing attendance at your local church is serving God somewhere else to meet genuine needs. Missing church to go on vacation, and to sporting events can be healthy; again, it depends on motivation and attitude. We are not saved by church attendance, but by grace. (Ephesians 2:8,9). In examining our motives for missing church, we should also examine our motives for attending church. Do we attend church to make ourselves spiritual? Or possibly for business contacts? Or do we attend church for the legalistic notion that says the more regularly we walk through the doors of the church, the more pleased God is with us? It's true that many people who attend church regularly do not have a good relationship with the Lord. We should desire to attend church so we can fellowship with others who have experienced the amazing grace of Jesus Christ. (Hebrews 10:24, 25).

We should attend church, not to collect spiritual bonus points, but because we love! We love His people and love His Word. Every Christian should attempt to attend church regularly. At the same time, missing church for a good reason is, in no sense, a sin; it should not cause feelings of guilt; nobody will go to heaven because they go to church!

The one entry to heaven is to accept Jesus as Lord and Savior! Without a personal relationship with Christ, religious words and religious ways, such as attending church, filling positions of church leadership, and performing good works, have no value. Jesus will say, "Depart from me, I never knew you." (John 14:6; Matthew 7:22, 23; Luke 13:25-30). Let us not make God's word to have no effect through tradition (Mark 7:13; Matthew 15:1-9). When Jesus' disciples came to Him concerning the religious hypocritical Pharisees being offended by His teaching, Jesus told them, "Leave them; they are blind guides. If a blind man leads a blind man, both will fall into a pit." (Matthew 15:12-14).

During COVID-19, my sons in the ministry: Sherman Witcher, Durwan Brewer, Shawn Thomas and Jonathan Davis stood with me in prayer and as encouragers. These men are born-again husbands and fathers. They made sure to keep morale up during this time. During the pandemic, many of our normal routines were interrupted; we were unable to congregate; therefore, we had to make changes. We had to have services via conference calls to continue having our Bible Study classes in conjunction with our community Bible Study Class that had been established in the past.

After the Covid-19, our community Bible Study moved to Erwin Community Center. Today, working alongside Brittany Witworth and Barbara Allison, two skilled orators and a community committee that helped to make the Community Bible Study Class (CBSC) possible. The numbers of our Community Bible Study Class have grown over the years, and we hope to see that number continue to grow. There have been several students in our Bible Study Class that have gone the extra mile to ensure I was fully prepared with all the tools needed to teach. Jonathan Kithcart is a brother in Christ and an assistant teacher for the community classes that are still held. We are always looking for new ways to grow and continue teaching. We currently have students that have joined our Bible Study Classes from many different states.

During Covid-19, in our Sunday School Department, we had a lot of instrumental teachers such as Minister Derek and Sister Sharon Funderburk, Sister Deniece Nichols, Sister Margaret Whisnant under the guidance of our current Educational Director, Minister Tangela W. Hinton.

To my beloved fellow Christian, as the apostle Paul stated, "I do not want you to be ignorant." (I Corinthians 12:1). After my beloved family: a note to my fellow followers of Jesus Christ - Why should you die before your time? (Ecclesiastes 7:17), as many did during the beginning of the deadly infectious disease caused by a virus Covid 19, beginning January 2020. I remember many warnings to not gather in assemblies or public places without proper protection, such as wearing a mask, or you could contract the virus and die. Leaders of some religious congregations encouraged parishioners to attend despite warnings of contracting the virus. Many parishioners attended because they were told that God would take care of them. I believe that with all my heart, but we must remember that God has given mankind knowledge about how to avoid gathering to prevent contacting a deadly disease as the Center for Disease Control Prevention (CDC) states. I do believe that God gave them the gift of knowledge about deadly disease (I Corinthians 12:8). Some of the leaders of the main branch of government communicated to the public that the virus was not as contagious as the CDC warned the public, and as a result, many thousands of people died. Hosea 4:6

highlights the consequences of rejecting knowledge and ignoring God's Word. Ignoring God's warnings will bring destructions, paying attention to God's warning will save a person from destruction. One of the responsibilities of Christians is to remind people of God's coming judgement and the way of deliverance is through Jesus Christ. (Romans 10:9, John 14:6)

Trials are Just a Test of your Faith – Faith challenges. As I look back on my Faith journey, I had questions when things began to look dark for me. I had heard many times that you should not question God. However, I was of an early age and not fully mature in my faith walk. It is not a sin to question God for clarity.

One of the faith challenges for my family occurred in 1984. My wife and I received the news that our oldest son, Tony, at 21 years old had been in a car accident and thrown out of the vehicle. This left him with a severe head injury. Can you imagine how devasting that news was for us? We learned that he had been flown to the nearest Neurological Trauma Center at Carolina Medical Center in Charlotte, North Carolina. He underwent an immediate four-to-five-hour surgery. All we could do was wait nervously. We were in prayer with our preacher, Pastor Worthy and my faithful prayer partner Deacon Willie Dunovant. The news finally came from the Neurosurgical staff, which was not positive or optimistic. The doctors told us that it would be a slim chance if Tony lived. Their terminology also said if he lived, he would be in a vegetative state. That is when our monotheistic faith became more elevated like never before, just like Abraham's faith.

Abraham believed that if he sacrificed Isaac, God would raise him from the dead. (Genesis 22:1-8), (Hebrews 11:17-19), "And with faith Moses told the Israelites to stand still and see the salvation of the Lord for the Egyptians you see shall not be seen, no more forever." (Exodus 14:13). My family and I took the unwavering faith route as these biblical Saints did in faith. After the surgery, our son was in a coma for a period of 5 months. My daughter, Jara, was very instrumental in the rehabilitation of our son. During the months he was in the coma, Jara would talk to him as if he could hear everything she was saying. She knew the precept of faith, "Even so faith, without works, is dead being alone." (James 2:17). The faith challenge continues, I could hear the Apostle Paul saying, "I have fought the good fight. I have finished the race. I have kept the faith and at the end of my journey the Lord will award me a crown of righteousness." (2 Timothy 4:7-8).

Our son's brain had been severed, and it left him without the ability to walk and use his left side, but by the grace of God and our faith in God and along with my family, God kept us. There were no head trauma facilities that we knew of in North or South Carolina. We were told the closest place that he could be treated for head injury would be in Tennessee, several states away. We began to pray and trust in God and, low and behold, we found out that there was a traumatic brain injury, rebound head injury facility in Lancaster, South Carolina. Tony started to have some mobility and was being trained in how to walk again.

Not long after he began to have a lot of movement in his legs and began progressing well, our Faith was tested one more time. We found out that the insurance had elapsed and he had been in the facility for three months without insurance before we were informed. We needed to try to find another facility for our son, but there were no other head injury facilities.

Without insurance, it was almost impossible to get the type of medical care that he needed. Our faith was tested when we left the Rebound Center in Lancaster, South Carolina; we were given a bill of ninety thousand dollars. To stay at the Rebound Center, the cost was thirty thousand dollars per month.

We had to get an attorney to investigate why the insurance had elapsed. God blessed us through our oldest daughter, Jara, who had graduated from "Winston-Salem State University with a degree in Social Work. She helped us to navigate through these challenging times.

Can you Handle What you Ask For? (Matthew 26:36-39; Luke 22:41-43)

Getting married at an early age is one of the best things I do believe that happened to me because it gave me a responsibility. I can still hear the echoes of my parents saying do what is right and I learned to take care of my family.

In 1996, my beloved wife, Jymmie, was diagnosed with Multiple Myeloma Cancer and passed away on January 9, 2010. When God blessed me with a wife and family, the ultimate trials began. At the time of her diagnosis, we had been married for 34 years. The life expectancy for this type of cancer was 14 years. Deacon Willie Dunovant was a devoted prayer partner to me during this time. Our pastor, Dr. Benjamin Hinton, along with many other people, prayed with and for us. We put our faith in God that my wife would surpass the life expectancy the doctors outlined for her, and we began the process of medical treatments.

My daughter, Jara, would stand along with me as we sought medical treatment from the top medical and specialty facilities in the state of North Carolina, facilities such as Bowman Gray and Wake Forest Medical Center in Winston-Salem, NC; and Duke Medical Center in Durham, NC. During my wife's treatment for Mesothelioma, we were thrown a curveball; she also developed a tumor in her head. Our loving family members and church family prayed nonstop for us. As I forementioned, it is okay to ask questions, but not okay to doubt God. "In everything by prayer and supplication and thanksgiving let your petitions be known to God." (Philippians 4:6). The tumor was successfully removed at Duke Medical Center. My wife had approximately twenty-eight surgeries; we went through excruciating days and nights. This had to be when I felt like I was at my weakest point in my faith walk. With all the overwhelming things I was facing, thoughts began to creep in to make me question my faith. I may have felt like it, but I could still hear the words of God saying, "I will never leave you nor forsake you." (Hebrews 13:5). I am thankful for God and His indescribable gift. (2 Corinthians 9:15).

At times, I began to feel uncomfortable, thinking that I may have abandoned the faith. The Holy Spirit led me to think about Jesus's struggle with His mission. Jesus made a covenant of Faith with the Father just as I had made a covenant vow of marriage with my wife. Jesus struggled and said to his father, "O my Father, if it is possible, let this cup pass from me." (Matthew 26:36). After seeing Jesus' struggle and God sending an angel to strengthen Him, the Holy Spirit strengthened me to keep the faith. (Luke 22:43).

Jesus made a covenant sacrifice to come into the world with a body made a little lower than the angels for the suffering of death for everyone. (Hebrews 2:9,18;10:5-9). After being led by the Holy Spirit to see all that Jesus did for me, it confirmed that I should keep the faith and the covenant of marriage and the duties thereof. Jesus said for this reason a man shall leave his father and mother and be joined to his wife. (Matthew 19:5; Genesis 2:24). Just when it seemed that nothing else could go wrong, another setback happened, and it overwhelmed my faith. My youngest son, Derek, passed away on May 1, 2023. Derek was a great educator in the Calvert County Public System in Patuxent, Maryland Appeal Elementary Campus. He was awarded the "Most excellent Teacher communicator to students" on conference calls during Covid-19 pandemic.

It was around this time that Derek was diagnosed with Multiple Myeloma, as well as Lupus. My son didn't want to burden me with his illness. He spoke every day with his sister, Francis Standfield, for hours as they commuted to and from work and at home. James Garvin, my son's best friend, would not miss a Saturday morning talking and praying with Derek for hours. James and Francis were so instrumental in encouraging my son during his illness.

It was truly a test of my faith when I received the call that my youngest son had passed away at the age of 53. For a moment, my faith seemed weak; and I was distressed and overwhelmed. Second Corinthians 13:5 tells us to "examine ourselves to see whether we are truly holding our faith." I remembered when Jesus made the covenant with his Father and said, "I will take on humanity for the suffering of death." (Hebrews 2:9). This was a true test for me, and the true test of faith is knowing God.

How to Cope when your Faith is Challenged

At this point in my faith, when James 1:2-5 said to consider it all joy when you fall into various trials, knowing that testing your faith produces patience. I remember this when I have a question, or I feel lacking in wisdom and understanding, especially after the loss of my beloved wife and son.

SICKNESS

I asked, "Why does God allow sickness?" The Holy Spirit led me to James 1:5. Sickness is always difficult to deal with, regardless of how strong your faith is. The key is that God's ways are Higher than our ways. (Isaiah 53:8-9). When we see our loved ones suffering with sickness, disease, or in the midst of a trial, it is very difficult to focus on what good God might bring about as a result. Romans 8:28 reminds us that God can bring about good from any situation.

Many people, as well as I, can look back on times when they grew closer to God. During those times, we learned to trust God more and how to truly Value Life; God knows the End Result. That is why my Faith is strengthened, and I thank God for His indescribable Gift. (2 Corinthians 9:15).

I write this for the future generation that's coming behind us, just as God commissioned Joshua 4:6-8, after the death of Moses. The dynamic truth is that hope of the future is based on the memories of the past, and this HOPE gives meaning to the present. (Joshua 4:1-7). I say to the future generation that's coming behind us: be strong, of good courage, observe to do according to all the law, do not turn from it to the right hand or to the left, that you may prosper wherever you go. (Joshua 1:6-7). TO GOD BE THE GLORY and may His peace continue to be upon you. (Joshua 4:19-24).

As this chapter closes, although the journey of forgiveness isn't always easy, I pray that this book illuminates the possibility of finding peace and renewal of the transformative power of love and forgiveness to each reader. I hope it reminds us that love guides the path with a renewed sense of peace and strength.
It is truly refreshing to know that success is color blind when we don't care who gets the credit. (Galatians 5:1). After being freed from the yoke of oppression, it allowed me to have a clear understanding and a heart of forgiveness that allowed me to see all mankind by the overall integrity of the heart.

My Legacy

Children: Francis Stanfield, Jara Smith, Frank A. McClure (Tony), Derek C. McClure

Grandchildren: Rachel A. Stanfield, William R. Smith II (RJ), Caleb F. Smith, Jamari McClure Hewitt & Jennifer Hall Allison

Great-Grandchildren: Amir Johnson, Amiyah Johnson, Cayden Makai Smith, & Reagan Smith

Final Prayer

My prayer is for God to provide strength to the men of the church. By having a strong spiritual foundation, you can grow into the person you need to be for your family, community, and yourself. The challenges faced by men can be addressed by relying on the strength and wisdom that God provides. A solid spiritual foundation, grounded in faith and guided by the principles of love, humility, and service, is essential for personal growth and for making a positive impact on those around you. The journey of faith is a continuous process of learning, growing, and looking to align your life with the teachings of Jesus Christ. By doing so, you can become a source of strength and support for your family and community, fulfilling your purpose and potential in this life.

After all the accomplishments, the greatest was BEING ORDAINED AND TEACHING THE GOSPEL OF JESUS CHRIST!

Special Recognition

In 1970, this young man, Derek C. McClure was being born while his father was playing in a baseball game. Frank's sister drove all the way to the game to let Frank know that his wife was in labor. Throughout the years, it inspired Derek to know that his father was in the middle of a game and left to go to the hospital to welcome his baby boy into the world. Derek collected and sent his father just about everything that had to do with baseball. Derek was an excellent educator with the Maryland School System for almost 30 years.

Frank is very proud of his collections from his son Derek. Frank's first check from bowling was in Raleigh, NC in 1977; he won $900.00 and finished Second out of 5,000 bowlers in the Men's Single tournament. With that start, Frank began traveling with Steve Werts, Bruce Brown, Sr., and many other great bowlers.

I am proud of my nephew, Dr. Darrell Johnson, who exemplifies remarkable determination in the pursuit of education. One memorable instance was when he arrived at a class late and was denied entry. Undeterred, he brought a chair into the hallway next to the classroom door and diligently took notes from there. His unwavering resolve led him to become a retired superintendent, highly sought-after as a motivational speaker.

As a motivational speaker, he traveled extensively across different states, spreading messages of determination and positivity. I had the privilege of going with him on some of those trips, seeing firsthand his remarkable achievements. Despite his success, he is still humble, often seeking my advice. My nephew had the honor of meeting with the 44th president of the United States, Barack Obama, at District 50 in Greenwood, SC where he was the Superintendent of Schools.

In moments like these, I am reminded of the Bible's wisdom: "Humble yourselves under the mighty hand of God, that He may exalt you in due time." (I Peter 5:6-7). I salute all my brothers, sisters, nephews, and nieces whom God has abundantly blessed. (Ephesians 3:20).

Special Tributes to Author

Uncle Frank is a man of God. First and foremost, he's on God's team. Uncle Frank leads by example. I learned the value of teamwork from him and my dad. He has shown all of us the importance of remaining faithful and working together for the greater good. I have been a practicing cardiologist for the past 20 years and I am certain my success as a physician has everything to do with this.

Extended version: My Uncle Frank is a great man. There are so many things that I can say about him. As the brother who was next to my father in age, Uncle Frank and my father (George) grew up being best friends. The McClure family was large. My grandmother had 14 children.

The importance of working together and teamwork were instilled early. Uncle Frank and his siblings knew from an early age that the success of one family member meant that all would benefit. It was clear that the success of the family was greater than the sum of the contribution of any individual. Made up of many naturally gifted athletes, the McClure family had many outstanding athletes. Uncle Frank was an excellent example. As a young man, he played Semi-Professional baseball. I have many fond memories of travelling from Baltimore to North Carolina and South Carolina to watch Uncle Frank play. He wore a white uniform with green and white stripes and a yellow hat.

I still remember his powerful hitting. Focused and sure, he was quick on second base and at short stop. He was constantly watching, looking at the runners on base, nodding to his teammates, talking very little. No one was going to get around the bases if Frank McClure had anything to say about it. My father was a teacher and coach for over 25 years. He coached his baseball team to the state championship in 1986. Nowadays in our family, Uncle Frank is known to be the family member who is the keeper of our history; he is the confidant.

For the last 20 years, I've been a practicing cardiologist. Having grown up around my Uncle Frank and my dad, I learned the tremendous value of teamwork. Working within the team concept is a governing principle in my life to this day. I am certain that my success as a physician has everything to do with this. Uncle Frank Is a man of God. First and foremost, he's on God's team. Uncle Frank leads by example. He has shown all of us the importance of remaining faithful and working together for the greater good. -Mallory L. McClure

Frank is my third brother. Being six years older than him, from an early age I was able to observe his tendencies and capacity for exceptional capability in sports. Frank's God-Given Gift as a spiritual leader and Bible Instructor has been evident throughout his life as he continues as a crusader to manifest his God-given talents for the benefit of mankind.

Extended version: Frank McClure is my third brother and the eleventh sibling in our family of fourteen children. Being six years older than Frank, I was able to observe him from an early age, showing tendencies and capacity for exceptional capability in sports! Playing Recreational Baseball was his passion! He first practiced the basics of the sport with friends and family in the yard and fields around our home where he always carved out time to play the game of baseball. Beginning as a teenager and on into adulthood, Frank played recreational organized baseball with city and county teams including York County, South Carolina and Gaston County, North Carolina teams.

Frank and his team players were catalysts who encouraged many young student athletes and other young people to accomplish what sometimes seemed to be unsurmountable tasks by "sticking to the tasks." Frank, individually, won trophies playing baseball which inspired and offered encouragement to a deluge of young people that knew him! While Frank's physical trophies and paraphernalia in his home tell the story of his love for baseball, younger generations of the family and community have been encouraged by him to appreciate their talents and to be a crusader for accomplishing their own dreams. Frank's exuberance in sharing his experiences about his adventures in baseball has also excited and ignited older friends, even the ill and despondent – offering times of laughter and hope.

Sometimes before visiting those who share his baseball passion (ill, elderly, etc.), he will call or send a message letting them know that upon his arrival they will be playing a baseball game! Frank would admonish

them to be ready to play their favorite position. The news of Frank's visit and the vivid memories of their days of playing baseball, plus the anticipation of the humor Frank exuded in his conversations caused smiles that indicated happy memories and great expectations of an amusing visit from Frank! Because of Frank's love for sports, before his late son Derek passed away, Derek supplied Frank with a stockpile of historic baseball and other sports memorabilia to cherish. Frank's God-Given Gift as a Spiritual leader and Bible Instructor has been evident throughout his life as he continues as a crusader to manifest his God-given talents for the benefit of mankind.
-Iola McClure

Our Community Bible School Class (CBSC) began with vision from Deacon Frank McClure through the guidance and spirit of God. Deacon McClure has a passion for God's people and sharing the gospel of Jesus by spreading the good news. He has led Bible classes at T. Jeffers Center and his church for several years. He has also been a guest speaker at churches throughout the community.

Deacon McClure reached out to some of his class members and shared his desire to continue the Bible study classes during the 2020 pandemic when churches, assemblies, and worship centers were closed for corporate worship. Through prayer and collaboration, Tuesday evenings were set aside for a teleconference Bible study class in place of the in-person Bible classes that Deacon McClure led prior to the pandemic. During this period, the teleconference call class grew exponentially. Over 40 participants called in from various states in the U.S. The class was, and is, non-denominational as there is no division in the body of Christ.

It is a community-focused group, and our mission is to help those in need through prayer, fellowship, and where needed, monetary assistance. Not only do we want to reach others through the word of God, but also through good deeds. When the effects of the pandemic began to subside, and people were allowed to assemble in large numbers again, Deacon McClure and his staff collaborated once again to resume the Tuesday in-person classes here at Erwin Center.

Since several students had joined from various states across the country, Deacon McClure also continued

to hold the teleconference class, now on Thursday evenings from 6:30 to 7:30 p.m. In studying God's word at the various classes, participants have raised theological questions that require additional time to discuss and answer. Therefore, this new question and answer class was established to allow for that time. This class will be held every third Saturday starting in July and continuing through December of this year.
-Brittany Whitworth

    Passionate, Knowledgeable, Steadfast. These three words capture the essence of a leader who believes in family. One of his most notable passions is his love for the game of baseball. Uncle Frank's knowledge of the bible is awe-inspiring. He has the innate ability to recite passages of the bible from memory. Mr. Frank McClure, affectionately known as "Uncle Frank", is the exemplar of someone who always seeks the best for anyone who is associated with him. He goes out of his way to make sure people are comfortable and able to function at the highest level. He is passionate about his family and makes sure that everyone is doing their best to be the best person they can be. In fact, he is notorious for asking tough questions to solve a situation yet is patient in allowing the person to respond with his/her answer. Whether he agrees or disagrees with the person is not as relevant as allowing the individual to decide on his/her own.

After retiring as a truck driver for years, Uncle Frank continues to drive throughout the Carolinas and across state lines to make sure his family is well, and he stands ready to assist wherever necessary.

Perhaps one of his most notable passions is his love for the game of baseball. Ever since I was a little boy growing up in Clover, I recall Uncle Frank being a key player in the hometown's African American baseball team, the Bowling Green Hornets. He was revered as a top player and one who was respected by teammates and opponents. Residents of Clover knew that Uncle Frank was on a mission to make sure that the Hornets were successful on and off the field. Whether he was playing third base or shortstop, batting third or clean-up, they knew that with him in the game, the Hornets had a great chance to win. He was dressed like a major league baseball player and had that winning attitude. He faithfully came to practice and encouraged others to work on their skills so that when game day rolled around, everyone would be ready for the task at home. On most occasions, the team was prepared and took care of business on the field and celebrated after the numerous victories.

Each week, people in town gathered around the pitcher's mound after the game to participate in the winning celebratory chant, often led by Uncle Frank. The chant, said in unison was: WE SHALL, WE SHALL, WE SHALL NOT LOSE! When those words were spoken more than 30 years ago, Uncle Frank always had a serious look on his face. Today, if those words are spoken, he will simply smile and passionately join in the chant.

Uncle Frank's knowledge of the bible is awe-inspiring. He has the innate ability to recite passages of the bible from memory. He has been an ardent teacher of the gospel and willing to discuss the bible and various passages with anyone. His Saturday Bible School class, as well as his classes at Tabernacle Baptist Church's Bible School, where he served as a deacon for more than 40 years, were always popular. He always had a question or phrase that he said, "wrinkled the brain" and required a little thought and research. He often would give the question in one session and close with the phrase "I'll give ya'll the rest tomorrow," and walk away smiling.

He was always prepared to assist with a bible phrase that would help a person address a particular situation. I'll never forget my conversation with him prior to accepting my first superintendent position. The job required me to pack up and leave home for the first time. It would require me to have courage to be successful. Although I was quite nervous, we had a conversation about the task, and he sent me away with a scripture that would help me complete this journey. The passage he shared with me was from Joshua 1:6-7. It was amazing how relevant this passage was, and his explanation was on point. Uncle Frank had the ability to engage in a conversation and make points that made you ponder for hours after the conversations. Three of my favorites include: "You would be amazed how much can be accomplished if no one cares who gets the credit for a job well done"; "Practice like you never won and perform like you never lost"; and "The art of an educated mind is the ability to entertain an idea and not accept it."

Uncle Frank is amazing…And then some!
-Dr. Darrell Johnson

THE FAMILY ALBUM

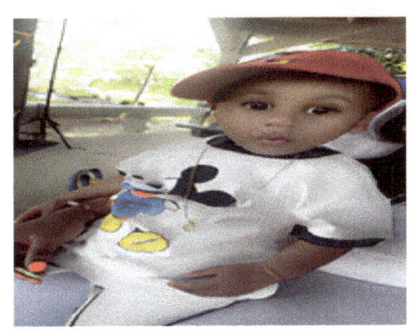

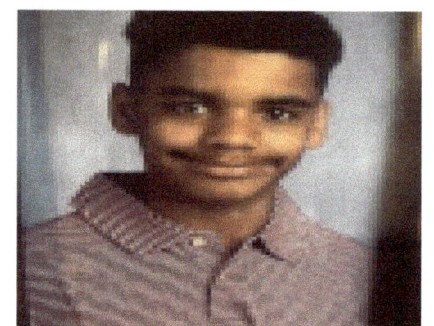

Victory With a Warriors Mentality | 95

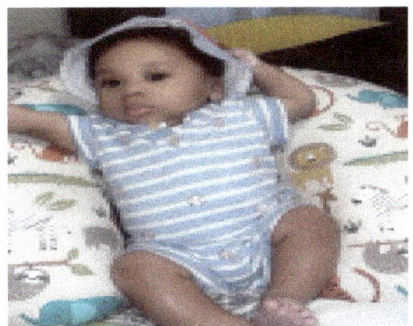